MW01282043

# Operation Ichigo

*A Struggle of Strategies and Alliances
in the China Theater*

Pacific Atrocities Education

# Operation Ichigo

*A Struggle of Strategies and Alliances
in the China Theater*

**Jillian Carrillo**

# Operation Ichigo

*A Struggle of Strategies and Alliances in the China Theater*

Written by
**Jillian Carrillo**

Editor
**Samantha Lee**

Published by Pacific Atrocities Education

Printed in the United States of America.

Paperback ISBN: 978-1-947766-67-9
E-book ISBN: 978-1-947766-66-2

# Table of Contents

# Introduction

The Imperial Japanese Army launched Operation Ichigo on April 19, 1944, with two primary objectives: the destruction of American air bases in China that supported Boeing B-29 bomber operations against Japan, and the establishment of a secure land route from Japanese-occupied territories in Manchuria and China to French Indochina. These goals were strategically significant for Japan's war effort, as they aimed to mitigate the threat posed by American air raids on the Japanese homeland and reduce reliance on increasingly vulnerable maritime supply routes. Operation Ichigo, the largest land campaign undertaken by the Imperial Japanese Army during World War II, involved approximately 500,000 troops. By October 1944, Japanese forces had captured significant territory, including the provinces of Henan, Hunan, and Guangxi.

The Imperial Japanese Army faced resistance from three main groups, albeit to varying degrees. The Chinese Communist Party contributed through guerrilla warfare based out of Yenan, while the brunt of the resistance came from the Chinese Nationalist military and American forces, particularly the Fourteenth Air Force led by General Chennault. Despite these efforts, several factors severely hampered Allied resistance. First, the structure of American policy in the China Theater limited their resistance efforts due to the United States prioritizing the European conflict over the Pacific. Second, deep divisions between the Chinese Communist Party and the Chinese Nationalist Party prevented China from presenting a united front against the Imperial Japanese Army, significantly weakening their ability to resist. This was compounded by the Nationalist Chinese Army's already diminished standing by 1944, which suffered from low morale, inadequate training, and insufficient supplies after years of continuous fighting since the outbreak of the Chinese Civil War in 1927. Finally, differing Sino-American political and strategic objectives further obstructed their resistance efforts, as seen in conflicts between Chiang Kai-shek and General Stilwell. These factors significantly undermined the joint Chinese and American efforts to counter Operation Ichigo, ultimately enabling the Imperial Japanese Army to achieve its objectives.

# U.S. Strategy in the China Theater: Europe First

The way American military strategy was structured in the China Theater limited any possible joint resistance efforts put forth by American and Chinese forces. American strategy was heavily influenced by Admiral Harold Stark, who served as the United States Chief of Naval Operations during World War II. On November 12, 1940, Stark wrote a strategic memorandum addressed to Secretary of the Navy Frank Knox.[1] In this memorandum, Stark outlined several scenarios and plans, labeled A through D. He ultimately recommended Plan D, leading to the document being nicknamed the "Plan Dog Memorandum."[2] The Plan Dog Memorandum became the foundation of the "Europe First" strategy that the United States employed throughout the war. Stark argued, "if Britain wins decisively against Germany we could win everywhere; but if she loses… while we might not lose every-

---

1. Gerard Roncolato, "A Naval Memo of Grand Strategic Importance," U.S. Naval Institute, May 2021, https://www.usni.org/magazines/proceedings/2021/may/naval-memo-grand-strategic-importance.
2. Ibid.

where, we might, possibly, not win anywhere."[3] Based on this reasoning, Stark recommended that the United States focus on a strong offensive in the Atlantic in alliance with the British while maintaining a defensive posture in the Pacific if the United States entered the war.[4]

This memo established a strategic foundation for American officers in their conversations with the British two months later. Staff conversations in Washington from January 29th to March 27th, 1941, discussed the ways the United States and the British Empire could defeat Germany and the Axis powers.[5]

Their final report, ABC-1, concurred with Stark's recommendation to prioritize the Atlantic and European area as the "decisive theater," relegating the Pacific to a defensive strategy.[6] Rainbow 5, the American military's updated war plan, incorporated the recommendations from the ABC-1 agreement and other input from British and American strategists into a detailed blueprint for global wartime operations. While it addressed multiple theaters, including Europe and the Pacific, it did not focus solely on the China Theater. Secretary of the Navy Frank Knox approved Rainbow 5 on May 5, 1941, and it was subsequently approved by Secretary of War

---

3. Memo, Stark for Secretary of the Navy, 12 Nov 40, p. 1, accessed from http://docs.fdrlibrary.marist.edu/psf/box4/a48b01.html on 25 August 2024.

4. Why "Europe First"?, accessed September 6, 2024, https://www.armyheritage.org/wp-content/uploads/2020/06/Europe_First_US_Army_Heritage_Final_Edit.pdf, 3.

5. Ibid., 4.

6. Ibid.

Henry Stimson on June 4, 1941. This plan formalized the "Europe First" strategy, which became central to U.S. military operations during World War II.

There were several reasons why the "Europe First" strategy was implemented, but the primary rationale was the belief that Germany posed a greater threat to the economic and geopolitical stability of the United States than Japan did.[7] Academics highlight four key factors: Germany's occupation of Western Europe disrupted transatlantic trade and threatened American economic interests, fascist Germany's autarkic economic policies were incompatible with American free-market values, German influence in Latin America was perceived as a threat to the Western Hemisphere, and the loss of traditional European markets for agricultural and industrial goods risked broader economic instability.[8]

Adopting this "Europe First" strategy heavily impacted American involvement in China and subsequent American strategy against the Imperial Japanese Army in the China theater. The main role of the United States was to keep China in the war through strategic advice and material assistance.[9] The idea was that as long as China remained in the war, Imperial Japanese troops would be occupied on the Asian mainland.[10] This meant

---

7. Ibid.

8. Ibid., 5.

9. "WWII Campaigns: China Defensive: U.S. Army Center of Military History," WWII Campaigns: China Defensive | U.S. Army Center of Military History, accessed August 17, 2024, https://www.history.army.mil/brochures/72-38/72-38.htm, 24.

10. Ibid.

that success was measured differently than in the European theater. Instead of building and deploying a fully effective Chinese military force to defend against the Imperial Japanese Army, American success was measured solely by keeping China in the war.[11] As a result, disagreements frequently arose between American and Chinese military officials over strategy and priorities. Key examples of these tensions include General Stilwell's clashes with Chiang Kai-shek over training and resource allocation, and General Chennault's disagreements with Stilwell over the role of air power in defending China.

---

11. Ibid.

# Tensions Rise between Generals in the China Theater

General Joseph Stilwell served as the American Chief of Staff to Chiang Kai-shek and commander of U.S. forces in the China-Burma-India Theater, giving him significant influence over U.S. military policy in China. For example, General Stilwell controlled all lend-lease aid to China. General Marshall picked Stilwell for this job because he spoke fluent Chinese and had substantial experience in China.[12] However, Stilwell earned a reputation for being blunt and difficult to work with, earning him the nickname "Vinegar Joe." He held a poor opinion of Chiang Kai-shek, whom he disparagingly nicknamed "Peanut" in his journal entries,[13] and expressed frustration with President Roosevelt, whom he reportedly referred to as "Old Softy."[14] Stilwell's disdain for politics and diplomacy, combined with his confrontational approach, strained U.S.-China relations throughout World War II, ultimately leading to his recall in 1944.

---

12. John E Shepherd, *Warriors and Politics: The Bitter Lesson of Stilwell in China*. DTIC, 1989, https://apps.dtic.mil/sti/tr/pdf/ADA517708.pdf, 63.
13. Ibid.
14. Ibid.

Tensions between General Stilwell and Chiang Kai-shek first rose during the Burma Campaign in 1942. Stilwell viewed the campaign as evidence that significant reform of the Chinese military was necessary to effectively counter the Imperial Japanese Army.[15] By April 1942, Japanese forces had overrun Burma, cutting off China from Allied supply routes and leaving it dependent on U.S. airlifts for military and economic aid.[16] Stilwell blamed the defeat on the incompetence of Chinese commanders and what he saw as poor military leadership within the Nationalist Army,[17] which he attributed to Chiang's decisions. Using this argument, Stilwell continued to push for reform of the Nationalist military, further straining his already tenuous relationship with Chiang. Their disagreements over military strategy and priorities would persist throughout the war.

In the spring of 1943, General Stilwell and Chiang Kai-shek could not agree on a strategy to liberate Burma from Japanese control. Chiang wanted a full-scale campaign to liberate all of Burma and restore the Burma Road supply line, while Stilwell advocated for a more limited focus on Upper Burma, which he deemed more achievable with the available resources.[18] Chiang also requested additional American airpower for the campaign, but Stilwell, frustrated with the Nationalist Army's performance and priorities, suggested that

---

15. Ibid., 64.
16. "Vinegar Joe and the Generalissimo."
17. Ibid.
18. Ibid.

Chiang ask Communist forces to join the fight against the Japanese.[19] This suggestion deeply angered Chiang, highlighting the ongoing tensions and mistrust between the two leaders.

Chiang Kai-shek adamantly opposed significant military reforms because they risked threatening the delicate political control he maintained during this time.[20] Conflict in China had begun in 1927 with the civil war against the Chinese Communist Party, followed by the Japanese invasion in 1937. Chiang was deeply concerned with keeping China unified under the Nationalist Party, dedicating much of his political agenda to limiting Communist influence. The close link between internal politics and military reform meant that creating an effective Chinese military would require sidelining internal political concerns, a compromise Chiang was unwilling to make.[21] General Stilwell's repeated requests for Chiang to enlist the help of the CCP illustrate his disregard for this political dynamic. As the war progressed, tensions between Stilwell and Chiang increased due to their conflicting priorities, further straining U.S.-China relations.

Chiang Kai-shek's consistent refusal to reform the Chinese military led General Stilwell to believe that leveraging Lend-Lease aid was the only way to push Chiang toward adopting U.S. strategic goals.[22] Stilwell

---

19. Ibid.
20. John E Shepherd, ibid., 64.
21. "WWII Campaigns: China Defensive: U.S. Army Center of Military History," 25.
22. John E Shepherd, ibid., 64.

recognized China's dependence on American aid, making this an effective, albeit controversial, tactic. However, President Roosevelt disapproved of this approach, fearing it would humiliate Chiang and undermine the Allied relationship. In a letter to General Marshall, Roosevelt wrote, "He is the Chief Executive as well as the Commander-in-Chief, and one cannot speak sternly to a man like that or exact commitments from him the way we might do from the Sultan of Morocco."[23] While Roosevelt resisted Stilwell's tactics, another figure was rising to prominence in the China Theater: General Claire Chennault. Chennault's focus on airpower appealed to Chiang, who increasingly viewed him as a preferable alternative to Stilwell's demands for ground force reform and offensives.

General Claire Chennault served as the commander of the American Fourteenth Air Force and maintained a close relationship with Chiang Kai-shek and his wife, Madame Chiang, which helped him gain their trust. He continually advocated for increased aid to the China Theater and had achieved several victories against the Imperial Japanese Army with his volunteer air group, the "Flying Tigers," prior to leading the Fourteenth Air Force.[24] Chennault was a vocal critic of General Stilwell and U.S. strategy in the China Theater, particularly Stilwell's focus on ground operations and military reform. This put him at odds with War Department officials like General Marshall and General Arnold, who viewed

---

23. Ibid., 65.
24. Ibid., 66.

his airpower-focused strategy as overly ambitious given resource constraints.[25] Despite these tensions, Chennault proposed a plan to use airpower to defeat the Imperial Japanese Army, which Chiang Kai-shek strongly supported—a level of alignment that Stilwell was unable to achieve during his tenure as the American Chief of Staff in China.

Chennault's plan sought to defeat the Imperial Japanese Army through increased air assaults against Japanese supply lines, shipping routes, and air forces.[26] Implementing this plan required reallocating resources from General Stilwell's program of reforming and equipping the Chinese military to fund the equipment, fuel, and logistical support necessary for Chennault's airpower strategy.[27] Chiang Kai-shek supported Chennault's plan because it avoided the politically sensitive and logistically challenging task of reforming the Nationalist Chinese military. Instead, the burden of offensive operations would fall primarily on American air forces, allowing Chiang to conserve his ground troops for other priorities.[28]

Unsurprisingly, General Stilwell adamantly opposed General Chennault's airpower-focused plan. He believed that airpower alone could not defeat the Imperial Japanese Army and warned that significant Japanese losses from air assaults would provoke a ground offensive

---

25. Ibid.
26. Ibid.
27. Ibid.
28. Ibid.

against American airbases in China.[29] In this assessment, Stilwell accurately predicted vulnerabilities that would later be exploited during Operation Ichigo. He also argued that reallocating resources to Chennault's air force would leave the Chinese Nationalist Army ill-equipped to respond to Japanese ground offensives.[30] Instead, Stilwell prioritized reforming the Chinese military, reopening the Burma Road to increase the flow of supplies to China, and pressuring Chiang Kai-shek to take these steps by leveraging Lend-Lease aid.[31]

Initially, President Roosevelt supported General Chennault's airpower-focused plan. However, by the end of 1943, his position shifted for several reasons. At the Cairo Conference in November 1943, and later at Tehran, Stalin's promise to join the war against Japan after Germany's defeat reduced the strategic importance of the China Theater. Additionally, the success of General MacArthur's Pacific island-hopping campaign offered more direct and secure bases for operations against Japan.[32]Roosevelt also grew increasingly frustrated with Chiang Kai-shek's refusal to take an offensive stance against the Imperial Japanese Army and his resistance to military reforms.[33] Chennault's plan, while achieving some successes, failed to deliver the decisive results it had promised, whereas Stilwell's Burma campaign was begin-

---

29. Ibid.
30. Ibid., 67.
31. Ibid.
32. Ibid., 69.
33. Ibid.

ning to show progress.[34] Most critically, Stilwell's predictions about the vulnerability of American air bases were realized when Japan launched Operation Ichigo on April 19, 1944. This major offensive destroyed key American airbases in China, preventing Boeing B-29 attacks on Japan and exposing the inability of the Nationalist Chinese military to effectively resist the Japanese advance.[35]

General Stilwell, Chiang Kai-shek, and General Chennault's differing goals and strategies caused significant conflict between the United States and China, creating ongoing challenges for joint resistance against the Imperial Japanese Army. These conflicts persisted during Operation Ichigo, complicating efforts to mount an effective Allied defense. However, before examining the culmination of these tensions during Operation Ichigo, it is crucial to understand the state of the Nationalist Chinese Army in the years leading up to the campaign. Chronic weaknesses in the Chinese military, including inadequate training, corruption, and low morale, posed substantial obstacles to American and Chinese resistance efforts.

---

34. Ibid.
35. Ibid., 71.

# Prelude to Operation Ichigo: Factors that Limited China's Resistance Effort

The Nationalist Chinese Army's resistance effort was hindered by the polarization of Chinese society and the poor organization and training of its military forces. This chapter will examine these two factors to provide context for the obstacles that arose during Operation Ichigo, which ultimately limited the success of the Chinese Nationalist Government and its collaboration with the United States.

Conflict over power in China began well before World War II. From 1927 to 1937, the Kuomintang (KMT), led by Generalissimo Chiang Kai-shek, and the Chinese Communist Party (CCP), led by Mao Zedong, were engaged in a brutal civil war for control of the country. Despite deep political and ideological divisions, the two parties were forced to form a temporary alliance to resist the Japanese invasion during the Second Sino-Japanese War. This uneasy partnership, known as the Second United Front, was primarily a pragmatic response to the shared threat of Japanese occupation. However, tensions between the KMT and CCP persisted, undermining efforts to mount a unified resistance against Japan.

This alliance was fraught from the beginning. Rather than forming a cohesive military alliance, the Kuomintang (KMT) and the Chinese Communist Party (CCP) operated independently, controlling different parts of China and focusing their resources on their respective areas.[36] The Kuomintang's wartime base was in Chongqing, while the CCP operated from Yan'an, approximately 500 miles to the north.[37] Officially, the Kuomintang was the recognized government of China during World War II, which meant that the United States provided aid exclusively to the KMT. Under the Lend-Lease Act, which allowed the U.S. to supply war materials to nations deemed vital to its defense,[38] the United States supported the KMT with air and logistical assistance, military advice, and technical support.[39] In contrast, the CCP focused on guerrilla tactics in Japanese-occupied areas, conducting sabotage operations and hit-and-run attacks.[40] These differing strategies, combined with their

---

36. "The Second United Front: A KMT and CCP Alliance in Name, but Not in Practice," Pacific Atrocities Education, n.d., https://www.pacificatrocities.org/blog/the-second-united-front-a-kmt-and-ccp-alliance-in-name-but-not-in-practice.

37. Theresa L. Kraus and John W. Mountcastle, "China Offensive 5 May – 2 September 1945," report, May 5, 1945, https://history.army.mil/html/books/072/72-39/CMH_Pub_72-39.pdf, 4.

38. "Lend-Lease Act (1941)," National Archives, June 28, 2022, https://www.archives.gov/milestone-documents/lend-lease-act.

39. Theresa L. Kraus and John W. Mountcastle, ibid., 3.

40. "The Second United Front: A KMT and CCP Alliance in Name, but Not in Practice."

separate areas of control, resulted in a fractured Chinese response to the Imperial Japanese invasion. The delicate and often hostile alliance between the KMT and CCP severely hampered China's ability to mount an effective resistance against Japan, as both parties prioritized their postwar rivalry over unified action.

The Kuomintang's resistance effort was also limited by poor organization and training of their military forces. Although Chiang Kai-shek's army consisted of 3.8 million men in 1941, it mostly consisted of poorly trained and ill-equipped troops.[41] Soldiers often lacked proper clothing, and malnutrition was common, particularly in under-resourced units.[42] Additionally, loyalty within the army was fragmented; most troops pledged allegiance to their unit commanders rather than to Chiang Kai-shek, further undermining centralized control and coordination.[43] The Nationalist Army's tactics also limited its resistance efforts. Prioritizing defense, Chiang's forces focused on conserving manpower and equipment rather than mounting large-scale offensives against the Japanese. This cautious strategy, driven by Chiang's desire to preserve his forces for an eventual postwar conflict with the Chinese Communist Party, contributed to the overall inefficacy of the Nationalist military response.[44]

---

41. Theresa L. Kraus and John W. Mountcastle, ibid., 4.
42. Ibid.
43. Ibid., 7.
44. "WWII Campaigns: China Defensive: U.S. Army Center of Military History," 7.

Chiang Kai-shek and the Kuomintang were preoccupied with concerns about the CCP and their movements within China.[45] Concerned about a potential postwar conflict with the Communists, Chiang held a significant portion of his army in reserve to prepare for this eventuality.[46] This decision not only weakened the Nationalist Army's resistance efforts against the Japanese but also strained relations with the United States throughout World War II. Although the United States provided substantial aid to the Nationalists through the Lend-Lease program, it quickly became apparent that the two allies had differing political and strategic objectives.[47] While the United States intended its aid to strengthen the Nationalist Army's fight against Japan, Chiang diverted a significant portion of the resources to stockpile for a future conflict with the CCP. This divergence in priorities contributed to a tense and often mistrustful relationship between the United States and the Nationalist Chinese government.[48]

Although the Kuomintang (KMT) and the Chinese Communist Party (CCP) had ceased fighting and formed a temporary alliance to resist Japan, fractures in this alliance prevented China from mounting an effec-

---

45. Todd Eric Janhke. "By Air Power Alone: America's Strategic Air War in China, 1941-1945." Order No. 1409836, University of North Texas, 2001. https://stmarys-ca.idm.oclc.org/login?url=https://www.proquest.com/dissertations-theses/air-power-alone-americas-strategic-war-china-1941/docview/304714150/se-2.
46. Theresa L. Kraus and John W. Mountcastle, ibid.
47. Todd Eric Janhke, ibid.
48. Ibid.

tive defense against the Japanese invasion. For example, Chiang Kai-shek insisted on deploying several of his best units to northwestern China to blockade the CCP in Yan'an.[49] General Joseph Stilwell reported that nearly 500,000 Nationalist troops were preoccupied with containing the CCP rather than defending China against Japanese forces.[50] This diversion of resources, combined with poor organization and corruption within the Nationalist Army, hindered their ability to launch coordinated strategic offensives.

As a result, Japan was able to consolidate its control in China, using it as a staging ground to support broader military aggression. By December 1943, five Japanese infantry divisions were redeployed from China to the Pacific islands, bolstering Japan's defenses against Allied advances.[51] Furthermore, while the United States provided significant economic and military aid to China, disagreements over how to allocate these resources hampered joint efforts. Chiang often diverted aid to prepare for a potential postwar conflict with the CCP, frustrating U.S. officials.

These underlying issues came to the forefront with the launch of Operation Ichigo in 1944. The Japanese offensive exposed the weaknesses of the Nationalist Army and posed a significant challenge to Chinese and U.S. forces, further straining their alliance.

---

49. "WWII Campaigns: China Defensive: U.S. Army Center of Military History," 7.
50. Ibid., 15.
51. Ibid.

# Operation Ichigo: Planning

By October 1943, the deteriorating situation in the Pacific made an overland supply route through China highly desirable for Japan. Allied attacks on Japanese maritime routes severely disrupted Japan's ability to transport critical resources from Southeast Asia, threatening its war effort. Establishing a direct North-South land route through China became essential for securing these resources, particularly oil and rubber, and sustaining Japan's military operations.

The growing presence of American air bases in South and Central China further motivated the launch of Operation Ichigo. These bases posed a direct threat to Japan, as they could be used to support B-29 bombing raids on the Japanese home islands. Neutralizing this threat became a top priority for the Japanese military. In response, the Imperial General Headquarters approved Operation Ichigo in early 1944, and planning and execution began shortly thereafter. The operation aimed to destroy the American airbases and secure the overland supply route to strengthen Japan's strategic position in the war.

In early 1944, Japan launched Operation Go-Go, a smaller campaign in southern China targeting Chinese forces in Guangxi Province. While this operation helped weaken Chinese defenses and secure positions for the larger Operation Ichigo, it was not explicitly a deception campaign. Instead, it served as a tactical precursor to Ichigo, contributing to Japan's broader strategy of neutralizing American airbases in China and securing an overland supply route to Southeast Asia.[52] The Japanese Southern Army conducted operations in southern China that led Allied forces to consider the possibility of an offensive targeting Kunming. As a key hub for the Allied supply line and the terminus of the Burma Road, Kunming was of strategic importance. However, the main objectives of the Japanese campaign during this period, including Operation Ichigo, were focused on securing a land route to French Indochina and neutralizing American airbases in central and southern China, rather than targeting Kunming directly.[53] Japan hoped to divert attention away from Operation Ichigo's primary targets through preliminary maneuvers and limited offensives. However, despite their efforts to maintain secrecy, Allied intelligence was aware of Japan's broader plans. By early 1944, Chinese and American forces had intercepted communications and received intelligence reports suggesting a large-scale Japanese offensive was being prepared, though the full scope and timing of Operation Ichigo were not entirely clear until the campaign began.[54]

---

52. DTIC ADA640839: Army Operations in China. January 1944 – August 1945: https://archive.org/details/DTIC_ADA640839/page/13/mode/1up.
53. Ibid.
54. Ibid.

# Overview of the Operation and Logistics

Operation Ichigo was divided into two major phases. The first phase, known as the Peiping-Hankou Operation or the "Ko-Go" Operation, began in mid-April 1944.[55] The primary objective was to secure the Beiping-Hankou railway (now the Beijing-Wuhan railway) to facilitate troop and supply movement.

During this phase, the Japanese Army advanced along the railway, defeating Chinese forces in their path and capturing key locations, including Yen-cheng (Yan-zheng) and Loyang (Luoyang).[56] Simultaneously, the 12th Army advanced towards Hsinyang (Xinyang) to secure traffic routes and open the railway for Japanese operations.[57] These coordinated efforts set the stage for the second phase of Operation Ichigo.

In Loyang (Luoyang), the Imperial Japanese Army defeated and destroyed the Chinese First War Sector

---

55. Charles F. Romanus and Riley Sunderland, *Stilwell's Command Problems.* Washington, D.C.: Center of Military History, United States Army, 1987, 319.
56. DTIC ADA640839: Army Operations in China. January 1944 – August 1945, 30.
57. Ibid.

Army, marking the successful completion of the Ko-Go Operation. Following this victory, the Imperial Japanese Army transitioned to the Hunan-Guangxi Operation, also known as the "To-Go" Operation, the second phase of Operation Ichigo. The To-Go Operation was divided into three key phases.

In the first phase, Japanese forces targeted the heavily fortified city of Hengyang, seeking to capture its strategic airfield. After taking Hengyang, the second phase focused on advancing to Kweilin (Guilin) and Liuchow (Liuzhou) to destroy the American airbases there, which had supported bombing missions against Japanese forces. Finally, in the third phase, the Japanese aimed to capture Nanning and reopen the Canton-Hankou (Guangzhou-Wuhan) railway, ensuring a continuous land supply route through southern China.

The Japanese forces in Operation Ichigo consisted primarily of the 11th Army, the Wuchang-Hankou Defense Army, and the 5th Air Army. The 11th Army included the 3rd, 13th, 27th, 34th, 40th, 58th, 68th, and 116th Divisions, along with elements of the Wuchang-Hankou Defense Army.[58] The Wuchang-Hankou Defense Army itself was composed of the 39th Division, the 17th Independent Mixed Brigade, the 5th, 7th, 11th, and 12th Independent Infantry Brigades, and the 5th, 9th, and 10th Field Replacement Units. The 5th Air Army played a crucial role in the campaign, providing aerial reconnaissance, ground support, and air superiority to facilitate the Jap-

---

58. Ibid., 32.

anese advance.[59] Additionally, Japan kept several divisions in reserve, ready to reinforce the 11th Army if the need arose, demonstrating their preparedness for prolonged engagements during the operation.[60]

---

59. Ibid.
60. Ibid.

# The To-Go Operation

Operation Ichigo began successfully for the Imperial Japanese Army. During the initial Ko-Go Operation, Japanese forces achieved rapid victories as Chinese defenses crumbled under their attacks, allowing Japan to capture key positions along the Beiping-Hankou railway. The swift Japanese advance deeply alarmed both General Claire Chennault and Chiang Kai-shek. Chennault wrote to General George C. Marshall, describing the situation as being of the "utmost gravity."[61] He warned that the Imperial Japanese Army would destroy American airfields in China unless immediate assistance was provided. Chennault argued that if the Fourteenth Air Force was supplied with a minimum of 10,000 tons of material per month, it could halt the Japanese advance. However, the chronic logistical difficulties of supplying Allied forces in China, exacerbated by the loss of the Burma Road, posed significant challenges to meeting his request.[62]

Amid the escalating threat of Operation Ichigo, Chiang Kai-shek urgently requested that General Stilwell

61. Charles F. Romanus and Riley Sunderland, ibid., 365.
62. Ibid.

come to Chongqing (Chungking) to address the crisis. However, Stilwell, preoccupied with the Burma campaign and its critical objective of reopening the supply route to China, delayed his trip for nearly ten days, citing ongoing operations as his priority.[63] As Stilwell postponed responding to the growing threat of the Ichigo offensive, concerns began to mount. Both Chinese and American officials, including members of Stilwell's staff, echoed General Chennault and Chiang Kai-shek's warnings about the gravity of the situation. Their collective fears underscored the significant risk that the Ichigo offensive posed to Allied operations in China, particularly the destruction of key American airbases.

On May 31, 1944, General Shang Chen, head of the Chinese Military Mission, delivered a message to President Roosevelt on behalf of Chiang Kai-shek.[64] Chiang warned that the Imperial Japanese Army aimed to seize control of the Canton-Hankou (Guangzhou-Wuhan) railway and destroy American airfields in China. In response to this growing threat, Chiang made four urgent requests. First, he called for the Fourteenth Air Force to be strengthened.[65] Second, he requested that gasoline, spare parts, and additional aircraft be provided to support operations along key railways and airbases.[66] Third, he sought to bolster the Chinese Air Force to complement American airpower.[67] Finally, Chiang requested

---

63. Ibid.
64. Ibid., 366.
65. Ibid.
66. Ibid.
67. Ibid.

the rapid delivery of 8,000 rocket launchers, each with 100 rounds of ammunition, to modernize and equip Chinese ground forces for effective resistance.[68] Chiang also summoned General Stilwell and General Chennault for strategy conferences to address the mounting Japanese offensive. These discussions highlighted the tensions within Allied leadership in the China Theater, as conflicting priorities and strategies often complicated efforts to mount a cohesive defense.

Phase one of the To-Go Operation aimed to capture the strategic cities of Changsha and Hengyang in Hunan Province. The Japanese first attacked and occupied Changsha before advancing toward Hengyang. Changsha was defended by the Chinese 9th War Zone, commanded by General Hsueh Yueh (Xue Yue), with additional resistance provided by the 99th Army, which fought in the Ta-Mo Shan hills to protect the western flank of the Japanese advance.[69] Yueh-lu Shan mountain was a key strong point for the defense of Changsha. This is where General Hsueh had massed his artillery to mount a strong defense.[70] On June 16, 1944, the Japanese 34th Division launched an assault on Yueh-Lu Shan while the 58th Division advanced on the city itself.[71] Despite resistance, Changsha's garrison abandoned the city between June 16 and 17, allowing the Japanese to capture it on June 18, 1944.[72]

---

68. Ibid.
69. Ibid., 372.
70. Ibid., 373.
71. Ibid.
72. Ibid., 374.

General Stilwell feared that the capture of Changsha would allow the Imperial Japanese troops to enter Kweilin (Guilin) within seven days. In response, Stilwell ordered the evacuation of British and American nationals from the area. On June 21st, 1944, hospital patients, missionaries, Red Cross workers, and teachers were flown out by air.[73] Following this, surplus personnel from the Infantry Training Center left the region by truck on June 27, as Allied forces anticipated the imminent fall of key areas in eastern China to the advancing Japanese.[74]

After the fall of Changsha, the Imperial Japanese Army advanced toward Hengyang, a critical target due to its location on the Canton-Hankou Railway and its status as the largest Fourteenth Air Force base in Hunan Province.[75] The 116th and 68th Divisions of the Imperial Japanese Army were sent to capture Hengyang. While the Japanese successfully captured the airfield on the 26th of June but the city itself proved much harder to capture, as it was heavily fortified and fiercely defended by Chinese forces.

The Japanese concentrated the majority of their efforts against the Chinese 9th War Zone Army, commanded by General Fang Xianjue, which mounted a determined defense that lasted over a month.[76] Their secondary targets

---

73. Ibid.
74. Ibid.
75. Raymond E. Bell, "With Hammers & Wicker Baskets: The Construction of U.S. Army Airfields in China During World War II," *Army History*, no. 93 (2014): 42.
76. DTIC ADA640839: Army Operations in China. January 1944 – August 1945, 32.

included Allied forces to the west of the Hsiang Chiang (Xiang River),[77] an area the Japanese sought to secure as route for communication and supply lines.[78] The 11th Army faced relatively little resistance along the rail line leading to Hengyang, but their advance was slowed considerably upon reaching the city's outskirts, marking the beginning of a prolonged and bloody battle.

Hengyang was defended by the Nationalist Chinese Tenth Army under the command of General Fang-Seien Chuech (Fang Xianjue), with air support from the Fourteenth Air Force.[79] Fierce Chinese resistance, combined with Japanese logistical difficulties, led to a prolonged stalemate that lasted over six weeks. Brigadier General Clinton D. Vincent's 68th Composite Wing of the Fourteenth Air Force played a critical role in hindering Japanese operations. Constant air raids forced Japanese troops to take cover during the day,[80] while nighttime attacks on motor transport severely disrupted Japanese supply lines, halting almost all logistical activities.[81] The Japanese cited several reasons for their unsuccessful attempts to capture Hengyang: difficult terrain, strong Chinese defensive positions, determined resistance, shortages of ammunition, and superior airpower of the Fourteenth Air Force.[82] However, despite these challenges, the 10th

---

77. Ibid., 43.
78. Ibid.
79. Raymond E. Bell, ibid., 42.
80. Ibid.
81. Ibid.
82. DTIC ADA640839: Army Operations in China. January 1944 – August 1945, 84.

Army was unable to capitalize on opportunities to attack Japanese supply lines, likely due to resource constraints and their focus on defense.[83] The city of Hengyang ultimately fell on August 8th, 1944, after weeks of intense fighting. The battle inflicted significant casualties on both sides, delayed the Japanese advance, and demonstrated the resilience of Chinese defenders, but it also marked a critical victory for Japan in Operation Ichigo.

The Japanese advance during this phase of Operation Ichigo faced significant logistical difficulties. Persistent air strikes by the Fourteenth Air Force targeted Japanese supply lines, slowing their progress.[84] Additionally, large portions of the railway south of Hankou were damaged and could not be repaired due to flooding in the area.[85] Despite these challenges, the Imperial Japanese Army pressed forward. This forced American and Chinese forces to make rapid decisions about defending key airfields near Kweilin (Guilin).[86] General Stilwell ordered bombs to be buried and detonated on runways to render the airfields unusable.[87] However, one airfield in Kweilin was reportedly kept operational temporarily to bring in additional troops.[88] Despite these efforts, both Kweilin and Liuchow (Liuzhou) fell to the Japanese on November 11, 1944, dealing a significant blow to Allied

---

83. Raymond E. Bell, ibid., 42.
84. Ibid.
85. Charles F. Romanus and Riley Sunderland, ibid., 399.
86. Raymond E. Bell, ibid., 42.
87. Ibid.
88. Ibid., 43.

air operations.[89] By this time, only the airfield at Nanning remained operational in the region.[90]

The third phase of the To-Go Operation focused on capturing the air base at Nanning. This move not only prevented Allied forces from launching attacks on Japan but also allowed the Japanese to establish a direct line of communication with the Southern Army. Portions of the 23rd Army advanced to capture Nanning, while the 11th Army secured vital points along the Canton-Hankou railway to reopen the route.[91] Other elements of the 11th Army moved to capture the airfields at Suichwan (Suizhou) and Nanhsiung (Nanxiong).[92] Nanning fell on November 24th, 1944, completing the third phase of the To-Go Operation and further consolidating Japanese control over southern China.

---

89. Theresa L. Kraus and John W. Mountcastle, ibid., 8.

90. Raymond E. Bell, ibid., 43.

91. DTIC ADA640839: Army Operations in China. January 1944 – August 1945, 34.

92. Ibid.

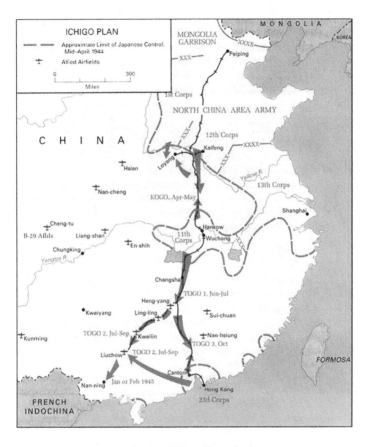

ICHIGO PLAN

Approximate Limit of Japanese Control, Mid–April 1944

Allied Airfields

0        300

Miles

MONGOLIA

MONGOLIA GARRISON

KOREA

Peiping

1st Corps

NORTH CHINA AREA ARMY

CHINA

12th Corps

Kaifeng

Hsian

Loyang

Yellow R.

13th Corps

Nan-cheng

KOGO, Apr–May

Shanghai

Cheng-tu

B-29 Aflds    Liang-shan

Hankow

11th Corps

Wuchang

Chungking

En-shih

Yangtze R.

Changsha

TOGO 1, Jun–Jul

Heng-yang

Kweiyang

Ling-ling

Sui-chuan

TOGO 2, Jul–Sep    Kweilin

Nan-hsiung

Kunming

TOGO 3, Oct

Liuchow    TOGO 2, Jul–Sep

Canton

Nan-ning    Jan or Feb 1945

Hong Kong

FRENCH INDOCHINA

23d Corps

FORMOSA

Source: U.S. Army Military History Institute

The Curtiss C-46 Commando was a vital American transport aircraft used during World War II, particularly in the perilous "Flying the Hump" operations, where it transported supplies over the Himalayan Mountains to support Allied forces in China, overcoming extreme weather, high altitudes, and enemy threats. Source: National Museum of the United States Air Force

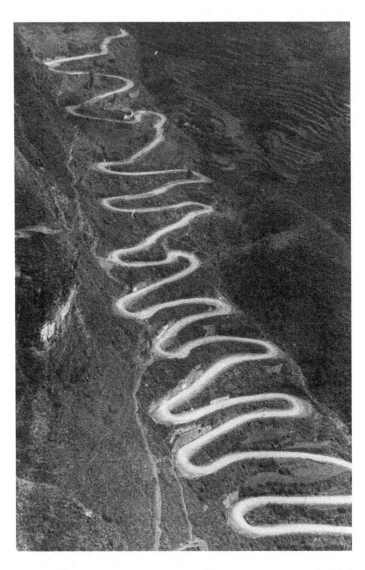

Until mid-May 1942, the Burma Road served as the primary supply route for Allied forces, but it was cut off when Japanese forces advanced westward through China to the Indian border, capturing Burma. Source: National Museum of the United States Air Force

Generalissimo and Madame Chiang Kai-shek and Lieutenant General Joseph W. Stilwell ("Vinegar Joe"), Commanding General, China Expeditionary Forces. Maymyo, Burma, 04/19/1942. Source: National Archives and Records Administration

Franklin D. Roosevelt, Chiang Kai-shek, and Winston Churchill at the Cairo Conference, 1943. Source: National Archives and Records Administration

Major General Claire Lee Chennault. Source: United States Air Force

Repairing a Flying Tiger P-40 at Kunming, China. Source: United States Air Force

Fourteenth Air Force B-24 Liberators on the line at Kunming Airport, China on September 6,1944. Source: United States Air Force

Japanese mechanized forces marching towards Luoyang.
Source: Yomiuri Shimbun, 14 May 1944

Japanese forces invading Henan. Source: Japanese Military Reporter

Chinese Army fought at West Hupei to protect their motherland in WWII.
Source: 中华民国史画

Civilians affected by Henan Famine in 1942. Source: Ifeng News

General Xue Yue 薛岳将军

# Chinese Resistance to Operation Ichigo

Although the Chinese Nationalist Government mounted a fierce defense against Operation Ichigo, their efforts ultimately failed due to a combination of factors: internal instability, conflicting Sino-American priorities, and severe supply shortages exacerbated by logistical challenges. This chapter will explore how these factors contributed to Japan's success during Operation Ichigo and examine the operation's long-term impact on China's political landscape in the years following the war.

Growing unrest among peasants, fueled by harsh taxation, forced conscription, and widespread food shortages, weakened the Nationalist government's control and undermined its ability to maintain internal stability during the campaign. Additionally, differing strategic priorities between the Chinese government and the United States hampered a coordinated response to the Japanese offensive. While the U.S. focused on defeating Japan, Chiang Kai-shek prioritized conserving resources for the anticipated postwar struggle against the Chinese Communist Party (CCP). Finally, severe supply shortages, compounded by logistical difficulties in delivering aid through The Hump and issues with corruption and mismanagement, left Chinese troops ill-equipped to resist the Japanese advance effectively. The failure to defend against Operation Ichigo not only inflicted significant military and territorial losses but also exposed deep weaknesses in the Nationalist government. These setbacks eroded public confidence in Chiang's leadership and contributed to the rise of the CCP, shaping China's political trajectory in the years following World War II.

During the first phase of Operation Ichigo, Japanese troops invaded Henan province, an area that had been suffering from famine since 1942. The famine was exacerbated by grain taxes imposed by Kuomintang General Tang Enbo on already struggling communities, as well as natural disasters and wartime disruptions.[93] In mid April, 1944, Japanese forces surrounded and captured Luoyang as a part of the Ko-Go Operation.

Local anger over the famine caused Chinese civilians to attack retreating Nationalist soldiers rather than resisting the Japanese advance.[94] Although reports that more Chinese soldiers were killed by civilians than by Japanese troops are difficult to verify, such hostility significantly hindered the Nationalist's efforts.[95] Additionally, the loss of valuable agricultural territories in Henan, Hunan, and Guangxi during Operation Ichigo deprived the Nation-

93. Parks M. Coble, *The Collapse of Nationalist China: How Chiang Kai-Shek Lost China's Civil War.* Cambridge: Cambridge University Press, 2023, 20.
94. Ibid.
95. James Chieh Hsiung and Steven I. Levine, *China's Bitter Victory: The War with Japan, 1937-1945.* Armonk, N.Y.: M.E. Sharpe, 1992, 172.

alist government of critical resources needed to feed its large military.[96] In response, the government imposed heavier grain taxes on the Sichuan province, one of its remaining strongholds, in order to make up for the loss created by Ichigo.[97] This policy further contributed to peasant unrest and discontent with the Nationalist party. The failure to garner popular support by Chinese civilians hampered the Nationalist army's resistance against the Japanese during Operation Ichigo as they often had to fight both Japanese troops and angry local civilians.

The poor organization of the Chinese Nationalist Military further limited the resistance effort during Operation Ichigo. Chinese troops relied heavily on traveling on foot, which restricted their mobility and made it nearly impossible to maintain flexibility while defending territory and resources.[98] This lack of mobility meant that Chinese commanders could not rely on reinforcements from other areas when their positions came under attack—a recurring issue during the campaign. For example, as the Japanese offensive progressed, the Chinese high command sent the Ninety-Third Army from Sichuan (Szechwan) to reinforce the Guangxi (Kwangsi) front. However, it took two months for the army to reach the front, by which time the situation had drastically deteriorated.[99] Throughout Operation Ichigo, Chinese commanders could not expect help from the National-

---

96. Parks M. Coble, ibid., 24.
97. Ibid.
98. James Chieh Hsiung and Steven I. Levine, ibid., 169.
99. Ibid., 193.

ist military in a timely manner. The gradual movement of troops also translated into sluggish transportation of supplies. Equipment and supplies had to be transported on foot because the government had no vehicles to spare.[100] The use of soldiers as carriers not only meant that supplies were transported slowly but also reduced the combat strength of the Kuomintang army units.[101]

In theory, the United States should have been able to make up for supply issues through the lend-lease program. However, after the closing of the Burma road in 1942, it was near impossible to deliver enough equipment, weapons, and munition to Kuomintang troops. Supplies had to be airlifted over the Himalayas (The Hump), a challenging and limited logistical route. As a result, Lend-Lease supplies often failed to reach units operating in the interior of China.[102] As a result, the lend-lease program did not adequately supply units in the interior of China. During Operation Ichigo, China only received 60 mountain guns, 320 tank guns, and 506 bazookas, the quantities were far from adequate to counter the Japanese offensive. Verified numbers vary, but historical accounts consistently highlight the insufficiency of these shipments.[103]Significant amounts of Lend-Lease supplies only began arriving in China in the late stages of the war, after the reopening of the

100. Ibid., 169.
101. Ibid., 171.
102. "WWII Campaigns: China Defensive: U.S. Army Center of Military History," WWII Campaigns: China Defensive | U.S. Army Center of Military History, accessed August 17, 2024, 25.
103. James Chieh Hsiung and Steven I. Levine, ibid., 171.

Ledo Road in early 1945. By then, Operation Ichigo had already concluded, and these reinforcements could no longer influence the campaign's outcome.

# The Culmination of Sino-American Political Conflict: The Replacement of Stilwell

Differing Sino-American goals hindered the Chinese Nationalist Army's ability to resist against the Japanese during Operation Ichigo. Both American and Chinese officials grew increasingly concerned as the Imperial Japanese Army continued to take territory in China. The U.S. War Department felt that the only way to combat this crisis was to place General Stilwell in full control of all Chinese forces. On July 3, 1944, the U.S. Joint Chiefs of Staff sent a memorandum to President Roosevelt, warning that the situation in central China was deteriorating rapidly. They expressed concern that General Chennault's Fourteenth Air Force would soon be incapacitated if the Japanese offensive continued unchecked.[104] The Joint Chiefs wrote: "The Chinese ground forces in China, in their present state of discipline, training, and equipment, and under their present leadership, are impotent."[105] They proposed placing

---

104. Charles F. Romanus and Riley Sunderland, ibid., 381.
105. Ibid.

General Stilwell in immediate command of all Chinese forces to address the situation. On July 6th, 1944, President Roosevelt followed the advice of the Joint Chiefs of Staff and requested that Chiang Kai-shek place Stilwell in full control of all Chinese forces.[106]

Chiang Kai-shek expressed agreement in principle to President Roosevelt's proposal to place General Stilwell in command of Chinese forces, but he raised concerns about its feasibility. On July 8, 1944, Chiang sent a letter to Roosevelt thanking him for his concern while emphasizing the unique political and military challenges that China faced. He wrote, "I like to call your attention to the fact that Chinese troops and their internal political conditions are not as simple as those in other countries… Therefore, if this suggestion were carried out in haste it would not only fail to help the present war situation here but would also arouse misunderstanding and confusion which would be detrimental to Sino-American cooperation."[107] Instead of immediately placing General Stilwell in command, Chiang Kai-shek proposed a "preparatory period" in order to help General Stilwell succeed in his position.[108] This cautious response aimed to address Roosevelt's concerns while maintaining China's sovereignty and avoiding political instability. Roosevelt was partially reassured by Chiang's willingness to discuss the matter but continued to press him to take the necessary steps to place Stilwell

---

106. Ibid., 384.
107. Ibid., 386.
108. Ibid.

in command as soon as possible, reflecting the ongoing tension in their wartime partnership.[109]

Chiang Kai-shek sent a memorandum to President Roosevelt on July 23, 1944, where he outlined three conditions that would have to be met for General Stilwell to be placed in command of his forces. The first was that General Stilwell could not command the Chinese Communist Party unless they agreed to obey the "administrative and military orders of the Chinese Government."[110] The second was that General Stilwell's position, authority, and title should be clearly defined.[111] Finally, he asked that the distribution of military supplies through the lend-lease program should be placed under the authority of officers in the Chinese government. Chiang Kai-shek argued that these conditions were necessary given the political situation in China and the "psychology of the Chinese Army and people."[112] He also explained that if the transfer of power to a foreigner was not carefully regulated, the Chinese military and people might think he was no longer fit to lead, potentially destabilizing his government.[113] This was especially critical given the delicate and contentious relationship between the Chinese Communist Party and the Nationalist Party. To facilitate the negotiations, the U.S. sent Patrick J. Hurley, an American diplomat, as an ambassador to mediate the transfer of command. However, progress was slow, and two

---

109. Ibid.
110. Ibid., 414.
111. Ibid.
112. Ibid.
113. Ibid.

months passed with little advancement. This delay fueled General Stilwell's suspicion that Chiang had no genuine intention of ceding full control to him, further straining the already tense Sino-American relationship.[114]

Setbacks on the Burma road caused Chiang Kai-shek to threaten to withdraw his troops from the North Burma Campaign. This threatened the success of the campaign against the Imperial Japanese Army. General Stilwell wrote to General Marshall about Chiang's decision, prompting a response from President Roosevelt. On September 16, 1944, Roosevelt wrote a blunt letter to Chiang, warning that China was "faced in the near future with the disaster I have feared."[115] He insisted that Chiang place General Stilwell in full command of Chinese forces immediately, arguing that "all your and our efforts to save China are to be lost by further delays." Roosevelt emphasized the urgency of the situation, reflecting his growing frustration with Chiang's reluctance to act.[116] The letter angered Chiang Kai-shek, who viewed it as an affront to his sovereignty and leadership. However, Stilwell did not take Chiang's vexation seriously and interpreted Roosevelt's firm stance as a signal that he would soon be granted full command. Confident in this belief, Stilwell continued his work, anticipating that the situation would soon be resolved in his favor.

On September 23rd, 1944, Stilwell prepared an agenda for a renewal of talks. He planned to go to Yenan to

---

114. Ibid., 442.
115. Ibid., 445.
116. Ibid.

speak with the Chinese Communist Party and discuss their acceptance of Chiang Kai-shek's rule and Stilwell's command.[117] Once they accepted this, Stilwell hoped to arm the Communist Party and send troops north of the Yellow River.[118] This marked the first formal American proposal to arm the CCP, although informal cooperation between the U.S. and the CCP, such as the Dixie Mission earlier that year, had already begun.[119] Although Chiang Kai-shek had originally agreed to work with the Chinese Communist Party if they recognized his rule, the impact of this potential cooperation can not be overstated. Throughout the war, Chiang Kai-shek did everything in his power to limit the Communist Party's influence and preserve Nationalist dominance. His reluctance to fully collaborate with the Communists reflected his broader strategy of prioritizing the postwar conflict against the CCP over immediate unity against Japan. Stilwell's proposal highlighted the ongoing tensions within the Allied partnership and the deep divisions within China's anti-Japanese resistance.

Chiang Kai-shek resisted arming his political rivals, the Chinese Communist Party (CCP), fearing it would signal weakness to his supporters and create a dangerous situation after the war. He also refused to place General Stilwell in command of Chinese forces, asserting that Stilwell was ill-suited for the "vast, complex, and delicate duties" of the position. Chiang claimed his deci-

---

117. Ibid., 451.
118. Ibid.
119. Ibid., 452.

sion was unrelated to President Roosevelt's urging but rather stemmed from concerns that Stilwell's appointment might provoke a mutiny within the Chinese military.[120] He also wrote: "General Stilwell had no intention of cooperating with me, but believed that he was in fact being appointed to command me"[121] and "General Stilwell is unfitted for the vast, complex and delicate duties which the new command will entail."[122] However, Chiang Kai-shek also reasserted his previous agreement that he would place an American officer in charge of all Chinese and American forces in China.[123] Chiang Kai-shek's message went unanswered for two weeks.

Chiang Kai-shek's message arrived at a period of change for the War Department. After Stalin pledged that the Soviet Union would join the war against Japan after the defeat of Germany, the United States had little reason to support a major U.S. effort in China.[124] This significantly diminished Chiang Kai-shek's bargaining power as "the China problem was becoming one of diplomacy and personalities, while the stiffening of German resistance ended the possibility of sending corps to CBI."[125] On October 5th, 1944, President Roosevelt responded to Chiang Kai-shek's request by agreeing to recall General Stilwell as Chief of Staff.[126] Three gener-

---

120. Ibid., 452.
121. Ibid., 453.
122. Ibid.
123. Ibid.
124. Ibid., 457.
125. Ibid., 458.
126. Ibid., 459.

als were considered for his replacement: General Patch, General Krueger, and General Wedemeyer.[127] Patch was commanding an army in France at the time, while Krueger was commanding an army in "a most difficult offensive operation."[128] This left General Wedemeyer as the only available successor to Stilwell. General Wedemeyer replaced General Stilwell as the American Chief of Staff to Chiang Kai-shek on October 18th, 1944.[129]

The command crisis in China caused a significant impact on all China operations, including the resistance effort against Operation Ichigo. Months passed while American and Chinese officials argued over who was fit to lead the Allied forces in the fight against the Imperial Japanese Army. During this time, the Japanese made significant progress in their Ichigo Operation, capturing key American airfields throughout central China at Hengyang, Kweilin (Guilin), Liuchow (Liuzhou), and Nanning. Meanwhile the struggle for command ensued between elite Chinese and American officers, the Nationalist Chinese Army struggled to survive and make any headway against the invading Imperial Army. This is clear in their lack of supplies, the sluggishness of troops due to factors like malnutrition, as well as the poor organization of the military. General Chang Fa-kwei, a Chinese Nationalist general, remarked that "the morale of the Chinese soldier was broken and he no longer had

---

127. Ibid., 469.
128. Ibid.
129. Ibid., 470.

the will to fight."[130] These weaknesses left the Nationalist forces unable to effectively resist the Japanese offensive, further undermining their position in the war.

---

130. Ibid., 467.

# Conclusion

Operation Ichigo was a tactical victory for the Japanese because they successfully captured major airfields in southern China and secured a land route connecting their holdings in Manchuria to French Indochina. This forced the Fourteenth Air Force to relocate approximately 400 miles west, reducing its immediate operational effectiveness and preventing American Boeing B-29 bombers from launching attacks on the Japanese home islands from China. The destruction of these airbases temporarily disrupted the Allied bombing campaign against Japan.[131] However, the success of Operation Ichigo yielded mixed strategic results for Japan's overall military agenda. While the capture of airfields in central and southern China achieved short-term objectives,[132] it spurred the United States to construct new airfields further west, enabling the continuation of B-29 operations from locations beyond the reach of Japanese advances.[133] Additionally, the capture of Saipan in the Mariana Islands Campaign in July 1944 provided the

---

131. Raymond E. Bell, ibid., 43.
132. Ibid., 43.
133. Sherry, ibid., 21.

United States with a critical base for launching sustained B-29 bombing raids directly against Japan. Unlike the vulnerable airbases in China, Saipan offered a more secure and logistically viable location for American air operations. From Saipan, B-29 Superfortresses could strike Japan with greater frequency and efficiency. The island's strategic position, approximately 1,500 miles from Tokyo, allowed for more effective deployment of American airpower and removed the reliance on ten-uous supply lines over the Himalayas (The Hump) to China. The capture of Saipan also marked a turning point in the Pacific War, as it gave the Allies a foothold for further advances, including the invasions of Iwo Jima and Okinawa, and paved the way for the eventual air campaign that devastated Japanese cities in 1945.[134]

The combination of continued B-29 operations from new bases in western China and the more robust capa-bilities afforded by Saipan largely nullified Japan's strate-gic gains from Operation Ichigo. While Japan succeeded in disrupting American air operations in the short term, the broader Allied advance in the Pacific undermined Japan's ability to secure lasting advantages. As a result, although Operation Ichigo had successfully accom-plished its goal of capturing key airfields, the opera-tion did not create lasting security for Japan. Operation Ichigo also overextended Japanese forces. The campaign required the deployment of significant resources and manpower, straining Japan's ability to defend its broader empire. By the end of 1944, many Japanese troops had to

---

134. Raymond E. Bell, ibid., 44.

withdraw from the territory they had previously secured during the operation to address other threats. This undermined Japan's ability to maintain its hold on the newly captured areas, particularly as the Allied advance in the Pacific increasingly shifted the balance of power.

The success of Operation Ichigo was largely due to several factors. American military strategy in the China Theater limited timely and effective support for China during the campaign. This was a direct consequence of the Europe First strategy, which prioritized operations in Europe and the Mediterranean over those in the Pacific and China. As a result, supplies, training, and troops were allocated disproportionately to the European front, leaving Chinese forces under-resourced and ill-prepared to counter the Japanese offensive. Logistical challenges, including the loss of the Burma Road, further hindered the delivery of aid to China, as supplies had to be airlifted over the Himalayas ("The Hump"), a costly and inefficient alternative.

Political conflict within China also significantly hampered the resistance effort. The Chinese Nationalist Party (KMT) had been in conflict with the Chinese Communist Party (CCP) since 1927. By the time Japan invaded in 1937, the prolonged civil war had already drained the Nationalist Army of strength, morale, and training. The eight years of internal strife left Nationalist soldiers exhausted and poorly equipped to handle a prolonged war with the Imperial Japanese Army.

Additionally, the Chinese Nationalist Party was often preoccupied with limiting the power of the Chinese

Communist Party with the hope of minimizing their post-war influence. Nationalist troops were often held in reserve for future battles with the CCP and Chiang Kai-shek repeatedly refused American requests for collaboration with the Communist Party. The lack of a united front against the Imperial Japanese Army caused a fractured military response to Operation Ichigo and led to a significant loss of territory. Similarly, the command crises and division between the United States and China further weakened the resistance effort. Disagreements between Chiang and American officials, particularly General Joseph Stilwell, over strategy, resource allocation, and command authority created delays and inefficiencies. This deadlock in decision-making provided the Japanese with opportunities to gain ground during Operation Ichigo. The combined estrangement between the United States and China, alongside internal divisions within China itself, prevented the Allied resistance from reaching its full potential.

The handling of Operation Ichigo had profound consequences for Chiang Kai-shek and his regime. Nationally, the operation contributed to growing support for the Chinese Communist Party (CCP) in the years following World War II. The loss of valuable agricultural territories in Henan, Hunan, and Guangxi severely disrupted the Nationalist government's ability to feed its population and military. In response, Chiang imposed heavy grain taxes on provinces like Sichuan, further alienating peasants and civilians. This economic strain led to peasant unrest, undermining the Nationalist Party's legitimacy and bolstering the CCP's appeal as a populist alternative.[135] The CCP capitalized on Nationalist defeats during Operation Ichigo to strengthen their position. They argued that the Nationalist government's failures represented international humiliation, particularly as other Allied forces were on the offensive elsewhere in the war.[136] Furthermore, the U.S. insistence on placing General Stilwell in charge of all Chinese forces unintentionally undermined Chiang's authority by implying that he was incapable of effectively leading his troops. This perception weakened Chiang's domestic standing and allowed the CCP to portray themselves as a more competent and united force.

In conclusion, while Operation Ichigo successfully disrupted American air operations and achieved Japan's immediate objectives, the campaign failed to deliver lasting security for Japan. The capture of Saipan and the continued Allied momentum in the Pacific rendered Japan's territorial gains in China strategically ineffective, exposing the limits of Japan's ability to sustain its ambitions on multiple fronts. At the same time, the Chinese Nationalist Party's response to Operation Ichigo had profound and lasting consequences on China's political landscape. The failure to mount an effective resistance against the Japanese offensive, coupled with internal divisions and economic mismanagement, eroded public confidence in Chiang Kai-shek's leadership. These shortcomings, alongside growing support for the Chinese Communist Party, ultimately contributed to the collapse of the

135. Parks M. Coble, ibid., 24.
136. James Chieh Hsiung and Steven I. Levine, ibid., 123.

Nationalist government during the Chinese Civil War, reshaping China's trajectory in the postwar era.

# Literature Review

Although Operation Ichigo was the Imperial Japanese Army's largest ground operation during World War II, primary and secondary sources are limited. The American perspective dominates the literature about Operation Ichigo, whereas primary sources from the Chinese Communist Party and the Nationalist Party are few and far between. The primary sources that do exist are written in Chinese and have not yet been translated into English. This issue also arises when doing research on the Japanese perspective. As a result, the majority of sources that are discussed in this paper are written by American military personnel or American historians, many of which were veterans. Although this paper has attempted to include a variety of perspectives, due to the lack of sources from China and Japan, the conclusions reached here are undoubtedly biased towards an American perspective.

For example, *China-Burma-India Theater: Stilwell's Command Problems* is cited at length throughout this paper. It is authored by Charles F. Romanus and Riley Sunderland and was published by the Center of Military History for the United States Army in 1987. Both authors have a military background. Romanus received his masters in History at the University of Illinois in 1937 before pursuing his doctorate at Louisiana State University. He entered the army in 1943 and was commissioned in March 1945. Romanus then became a historical officer in the headquarters of the China Theater. After the war, he became a historian for the Historical Section of the Office of the Quartermaster General. Sunderland was called to active duty as a second lieutenant in the Field Artillery in April 1942. From July 1945 to May 1946, he served in the Historical Section headquarters in the India-Burma Theater. After the war, Sunderland became a senior operations research analyst for Technical Operations in Arlington, Massachusetts. These authors were undoubtedly shaped by their experiences in the China-India-Burma Theater.

Their research was comprehensive and utilized an abundance of primary sources. The majority of these sources are correspondences between senior American and Chinese officials. For example, they cite several memorandums between President Roosevelt and Chiang Kai-shek. The authors also utilize General Stilwell's diary in order to infer what the general was thinking at any given time. This was particularly useful when Chiang Kai-shek requested the recall of General Stilwell in 1944. However, they rarely cite Japanese sources and their Chinese sources are largely limited to memos written by Chiang Kai-shek and his staff members. Given this and their experiences within the United States military in the China Theater throughout World War II, their analyses of the events are likely biased towards an American perspective. This has significantly shaped the historical narrative by perpetuating the idea that Chiang Kai-shek and the Nationalist military were useless throughout the war.

The monograph *Army Operations in China: January 1944 – August 1945* was also cited at length throughout this paper. This source was particularly helpful in providing detailed information about the planning and execution of Operation Ichigo. This was an interesting source because it combined both Japanese and American perspectives. It was prepared under instructions from the Supreme Commander for the Allied Powers to the Japanese Government. The original studies were written by former Japanese Army and Navy officers under the supervision of the Historical Records Section of the First Army and Second Navy Demobilization Bureaus of the Japanese Government. The studies were then translated from Japanese into English by the Military Intelligence Service Group. After translation, the manuscript was heavily edited by the Japanese Research Division of the Office of the Military History Headquarters. Although the source was originally written in Japanese by former Japanese officers, it was translated into English and then edited by an American Military group. Translation and editing always run the risk of bias and misinterpretation.

The writers have admitted several blind spots themselves, pointing to the lack of operational records that are normally used as sources for this type of study.[137] They explain that "many official orders, plans and unit journals were lost during field operations and bombing raids or were destroyed at the cessation of hostilities."[138] However, they add that the majority of orders have been reconstructed in the report based on the memory of Japanese military officers. This is their justification for the extensive research done by the Japanese Research Division in order to validate the information, check the dates, and to add important data. The nature of this report is interesting as it details the perspective of the Imperial Japanese Army, however, it has been heavily edited and adapted by American military historians. The monograph was incredibly useful for dates, locations, and objectives, but, unfortunately, it is the only translated source that was easily accessible and was so heavily influenced by American military personnel.

These are just two examples of sources that are used throughout this paper. However, these sources share a common theme with the other sources included in this work: they rely heavily on the work of American historians and veterans. As a result, further research is needed on the Chinese and Japanese perspectives during Operation Ichigo. It is essential for the researcher to know how to read Chinese or Japanese before delving into Chinese and Japanese archives before arriving at a conclusion or forming an opinion.

---

137. DTIC ADA640839: Army Operations in China. January 1944 – August 1945, 3.
138. Ibid.

# Bibliography

## Primary Sources

"Army Operations in China. January 1944 – August 1945."
Defense Technical Information Center, August 31, 1956.
https://archive.org/details/DTIC_ADA640839/page/3/
mode/1up.

Stark, Harold. "Memorandum for the Secretary." FDR Libra-
ry, November 12, 1940. http://docs.fdrlibrary.marist.edu/
psf/box4/a48b01.html.

## Secondary Sources

Bell, Raymond E. "With Hammers & Wicker Baskets: The
Construction of U.S. Army Airfields in China During
World War II." *Army History*, no. 93 (2014): 30-54.
http://www.jstor.org/stable/26300287.

Coble, Parks M. *The Collapse of Nationalist China: How Chiang Kai-shek Lost China's Civil War*. Cambridge: Cambridge University Press, 2023.

Hsiung, James Chieh, and Steven I. Levine. *China's Bitter Victory: The War with Japan, 1937-1945*, Armonk, N.Y.: M.E. Sharpe, 1992.

Jahnke, Todd Eric. "By Air Power Alone: America's Strategic Air War in China, 1941-1945." Order No. 1409836, University of North Texas, 2001. https://stmarys-ca.idm.oclc.org/login?url=https://www.proquest.com/dissertations-theses/air-power-alone-americas-strategic-war-china-1941/docview/304714150/se-2.

Kraus, Theresa L. *China offensive*. Washington, DC: U.S. Army Center of Military History, Supt. of Docs, 1996.

Kuo, Tai-Chun, Hsiao-ting Lin, and Ramon H Myers. "Vinegar Joe and the Generalissimo." Hoover Institution, July 30, 2005. https://www.hoover.org/research/vinegar-joe-and-generalissimo.

"Lend-Lease Act (1941)." National Archives and Records Administration. Accessed September 13, 2024. https://www.archives.gov/milestone-documents/lend-lease-act.

Maroulis, Sophia. "The Second United Front: A KMT and CCP Alliance in Name, but Not in Practice." Pacific Atrocities Education, August 8, 2022. https://www.pacificatrocities.org/blog/the-second-united-front-a-kmt-and-ccp-alliance-in-name-but-not-in-practice.

"Marshall and the Recall of Stilwell." The George C. Marshall Foundation, October 18, 2018. https://www.marshallfoundation.org/articles-and-features/marshall-and-the-recall-of-stilwell/.

Romanus, Charles F., and Riley Sunderland. *Stilwell's Command Problems*. Washington, D.C.: Center of Military History, United States Army, 1987.

Roncolato, Gerard D. "A Naval Memo of Grand Strategic Importance." U.S. Naval Institute, May 2021. https://www.usni.org/magazines/proceedings/2021/may/naval-memo-grand-strategic-importance.

Shepherd, John E. *Warriors and Politics: The Bitter Lesson of Stilwell in China*. DTIC, 1989. https://apps.dtic.mil/sti/tr/pdf/ADA517708.pdf.

"Why 'Europe First'? The Cultural, Economic and Ideological Underpinnings of America's 'Europe First' Strategy, 1940-1941." Army Heritage Center Foundation. Accessed September 14, 2024. https://www.armyheritage.org/wp-content/uploads/2020/06/Europe_First_US_Army_Heritage_Final_Edit.pdf.

"WWII Campaigns: China Defensive: U.S. Army Center of Military History." WWII Campaigns: China Defensive | U.S. Army Center of Military History. Accessed August 17, 2024. https://www.history.army.mil/brochures/72-38/72-38.htm.

Made in the USA
Las Vegas, NV
04 April 2025

20537153R00046